AF487792

Whispers of Wisdom

Tales That Touch the Soul

Author: Unknown
Drafted by: SGMaxout

WHISPERS OF WISDOM

TALES THAT TOUCH THE SOUL

We are all storytellers. From ancient times around a fire to quiet bedtime whispers, stories have carried our truths, lessons, and dreams. In this small collection, you will discover tales that may make you smile, think, reflect, or simply pause. They come from different walks of life, yet each one carries a spark — a whisper of wisdom.

These stories are not bound by culture, religion, or age. They are timeless, simple, and profound in the way only true stories can be.

Author: Our Grandma's & Grandpa's
Drafted by: SGMaxout

① RABIT & DOG

It was a hot afternoon, and a hungry dog wandered through the forest. His stomach growled with hunger as he sniffed the ground and searched for something to eat. He hadn't eaten in a long time and was growing weaker by the minute.

Just then, his eyes caught a glimpse of a small rabbit nibbling on some grass. "Ah, finally!" the dog thought. "That rabbit will make a perfect meal." Without a second thought, he sprang into action, barking loudly and sprinting after the rabbit.

Startled, the rabbit looked up and saw the dog charging toward him. With no time to lose, the rabbit bolted into the bushes. He darted through the trees, leaped over rocks, and squeezed through narrow paths, with the dog close behind. The dog chased the rabbit with all the energy he had, but no matter how fast he ran, the rabbit always stayed just out of reach. After a long, exhausting chase, the dog finally gave up. Panting and tired, he sat down and called out, "Rabbit! How did you escape me? I'm bigger, stronger, and faster than you!" The rabbit, still catching his breath, turned around and replied, "You were running for your lunch. I was running for my life. That's the difference." The dog paused and thought deeply about what the rabbit had said.

Moral of the Story:
When you have a powerful reason—when your goal truly matters—you will give everything you've got. Purpose gives strength, focus, and determination. A clear reason fuels unstoppable effort.

One quiet afternoon, a weary traveler was passing through a sleepy little village. As he strolled down a dusty road, he noticed an old wooden house with a porch shaded by tall, swaying trees. Resting on that porch was a dog, letting out long, sorrowful howls that echoed into the stillness.

The traveler stopped, concerned by the sound of the animal's distress. He turned to an old man rocking gently in a chair nearby.

"Excuse me," the traveler asked kindly, "why is your dog crying like that?"

The old man didn't even pause his gentle rocking. With a calm voice, he replied, "Oh, he's lying on a nail."

The traveler blinked in surprise. "On a nail? Then why doesn't he get up and move?"

The old man gave a small shrug and said, "Well, I suppose it just doesn't hurt quite enough yet."

The traveler stood in silence for a moment, digesting the words. He glanced again at the dog, still moaning softly, unwilling to rise.

As he walked away, the traveler carried the image with him. He couldn't help but think about how often people—just like that dog—stay stuck in discomfort or pain. Not because they have to, but because it's easier to suffer a little than to make the effort to change.

🐾 Moral of the Story:

Sometimes we stay in uncomfortable situations because it's easier than changing.

But when the pain becomes **too big to ignore—** That's when we finally decide to change.

Don't wait too long— be brave and make a change when you need to.

Once upon a time, by the shore of a vast and powerful sea, there lived a tiny sparrow with her beloved chicks. Her days were filled with joy as she fed and cared for them in their snug little nest nestled near the sand dunes.

But one fateful day, as the sparrow soared into the sky in search of food, the waves turned wild and fierce. A huge wave rose like a mountain and crashed onto the shore. When the sparrow returned, her nest was gone—and so were her babies. The sea had taken them.

The tiny sparrow let out a cry that echoed across the beach. Her heart burned with sorrow and anger. Standing at the edge of the ocean, she stared into its vast, endless depths and shouted,

"You have taken my children! I will not rest until I get them back. I will dry you up—drop by drop if I must!"

The sea, deep and endless, chuckled with amusement.

"You? Dry me? You are just a tiny bird. How could you possibly defeat me?"

But the sparrow was not discouraged. Without hesitation, she flew down, dipped her beak into the water, and carried a single drop away. Again and again, she repeated this—one drop at a time.

The other animals gathered and laughed.
"What difference can you make?" they mocked.
But the sparrow calmly replied, "I'm doing my part."
Day turned into night. Still, she continued. Her wings ached, her feathers drooped, but her spirit did not waver. She had made a promise—to herself, to her children, and to the sea.
Moved by her unshakable resolve, a whisper of admiration spread across the forest. Word of her bravery reached the skies, and soon, the mighty Eagle, king of all birds, flew down beside her.
"You are not alone anymore," he declared.

With a single cry from the eagle, flocks of birds from every corner of the land came to help the tiny sparrow.

Seeing this, the sea trembled. For the first time, it felt fear. This was no longer a fight of strength, but of determination, unity, and purpose.

Afraid of what might come next, the sea relented. With a great wave that gently kissed the shore, it returned the sparrow's chicks, safe and unharmed.

Tears of joy filled the sparrow's eyes. She had done what seemed impossible—because she believed, and she acted.

MORAL OF THE STORY:

When your reason is clear and your heart is true, the size of the challenge doesn't matter. Even the smallest efforts, when fueled by purpose, can move mountains— and the universe itself will rise to support you.

4 THE MONKEY AND THE PEANUTS

Once upon a time, in a quiet village near the edge of a forest, a young monkey spotted a shiny glass jar filled with peanuts. The jar had a narrow neck, just wide enough for his hand to slide in.

Greedy with excitement, the monkey reached inside and grabbed a large handful of peanuts. But when he tried to pull his fist out—he couldn't. The jar's neck was too narrow for his clenched fist. All he had to do was let go... but he wouldn't.

He tugged and twisted, grunted and growled, refusing to loosen his grip. He wanted all the peanuts.

While he struggled, a man who had set the trap quietly crept up behind him. Within moments, the monkey was captured.

That man was a street performer. He trained animals to do tricks for coins and applause. He gave the monkey a name, taught him how to dance, spin, salute, and even wear little costumes. And each time the monkey followed orders, he was rewarded—with just a few peanuts.

Over time, the monkey got used to this life. The cheers of the crowd, the praise of the master, and the ever-faithful reward of peanuts after each performance. He stopped thinking about the forest or freedom. He stopped using his own instincts and lived only for the next peanut.

Years passed. The monkey grew older. He was slower now, less agile, less amusing to the crowd. He could no longer perform the tricks like he once did. But by then, his daily peanuts were many—more than ever before.
The master, watching closely, did some quick thinking.
"For the same peanuts I give this old monkey, I could train two younger ones. More energy, more shows, more money." And so, one morning, the master opened the monkey's cage and let him go.
The old monkey wandered the streets, confused and broken. The crowd that once clapped now passed him by. He went from one showman to another, begging to be taken in. But his tricks were outdated. His skills were worn. And no one had time for an old monkey with nothing new to offer.

Moral of the story:

This is the tale of many who enter the comforts of a system—trading time, skills, and freedom for small rewards. Over time, they forget their own purpose, their instincts, and their potential. And when they are no longer "useful," they are replaced.

The lesson? Don't just work for peanuts. Build your own path. Never stop learning, growing, and remembering who you were before the jar.

THE LION AND THE HUNTER

In the heart of Africa's wild savannas, where golden grasslands stretch endlessly and danger hides in the shadows, there arrived a man known far and wide—Shambhu Shikari. He was a legendary hunter, fearless and proud, with dozens of trophies to his name. But now, he had come seeking his biggest prize yet: an African lion.

For days, he roamed the plains, stalking tracks, listening to roars in the distance, watching the winds for signs. Finally, on a blazing hot afternoon, he saw it—a mighty lion, regal and fierce, standing tall near a rocky outcrop.

Their eyes met.

The hunter raised his rifle without hesitation and fired.

Bang!

But the lion, swift as a shadow, dodged the bullet and charged straight at him. Shambhu remained calm, quickly reloading. He aimed again and fired a second shot.

Bang!

Again, the lion swerved with power and grace, and this time, it ran even faster, roaring thunderously as it closed the distance.

Suddenly, the fearless hunter's hands began to shake. This wasn't going according to his plan.

He turned and ran.

Through tall grass and dry shrubs, he sprinted, heart pounding, breath heaving. But no matter how fast he ran, the lion chased with terrifying speed.

Moments later, Shambhu reached a cliff's edge, where below a raging river flowed far beneath. The drop was steep—almost certain death. But behind him, he heard the lion's growl drawing closer.

He was trapped.

Sweat rolled down his face. His mind raced.

"If I stand here, the lion will surely kill me.

If I jump, I might die… but maybe… just maybe… I might survive."

And then, in that split second—without time to calculate, to weigh the odds, or to fear—he jumped.

Moments later, Shambhu reached a cliff's edge, where below a raging river flowed far beneath. The drop was steep —almost certain death. But behind him, he heard the lion's growl drawing closer.

He was trapped.

Sweat rolled down his face. His mind raced.

"If I stand here, the lion will surely kill me.

If I jump, I might die… but maybe… just maybe… I might survive."

And then, in that split second—without time to calculate, to weigh the odds, or to fear—he jumped.

Moral of the Story

In life, there come moments when we stand at the edge—with danger behind us and uncertainty ahead. At those times, staying where we are guarantees failure. The only way forward is to take a leap of faith. Sometimes, taking the risk is the only chance we have to survive—and to grow.

When the situation demands it, dare to jump.

THE WOODCUTTER

There was a woodcutter who spent his days in the forest, chopping down trees with all his might. His axe swung with force, and his arms ached from the constant effort. However, despite his relentless work, he seemed to be making very little progress. The pile of felled trees remained small, and his work felt never-ending.

A passerby, noticing the woodcutter's struggle, approached and asked, "Why don't you take a moment to sharpen your axe? It would make your task much easier."

The woodcutter paused for a moment, wiped the sweat from his brow, and quickly replied, "I can't afford the time to sharpen my axe. I've got too much work to do. I'm busy cutting trees."

The passerby looked at him thoughtfully and said, "But if you sharpened your axe, you would be able to cut more trees with less effort and in less time. It would be a smarter approach, wouldn't it?"

The woodcutter shook his head, too focused on his immediate task to listen. He believed that working harder was the solution to his problems, but in reality, the key to his success lay in working smarter, not harder.

Moral:

Sometimes, we get so caught up in the hustle and bustle of our tasks that we forget the importance of taking a step back and preparing ourselves for greater efficiency. Working smarter—by sharpening our tools, learning new skills, or reassessing our approacch— can often lead to much better results than just working harder.

Once upon a time, in a peaceful meadow, there lived three little pigs who loved to play together. Their favorite pastime was rolling in the mud, squealing with joy as they splashed about. Life was simple and fun, and the three friends were content in their routine.

One sunny afternoon, as they were busy playing in their favorite muddy spot, a beautiful angel appeared from the sky. She glowed with a warm, radiant light, and the pigs stopped in awe to look at her.

The angel smiled gently and said, "Dear little pigs, tomorrow at sunset, if you jump into the small river that flows just beyond the hill, something magical will happen. You will be transformed into angels, just like me." The pigs gasped in wonder. "Really?" one asked excitedly.

"Yes," the angel replied. "But only if you truly believe and take the leap." And with that, she vanished into the sky, leaving behind a trail of light. That night, the three pigs couldn't stop talking about what had happened. Two of them were buzzing with excitement, dreaming about flying, glowing, and living among the stars.

But the third pig was quiet, unsure whether he believed the angel's words. The next day, as the sun began to dip behind the hills, the two eager pigs stood beside the river, their eyes shining with anticipation. "Come on!" they called to their friend, who stood at a distance, hesitating.

"No," the third pig said slowly. "What if she was just joking? What if it's a trick? I don't want to look foolish."

The other two gave him one last hopeful glance, then, smiling brightly, they jumped into the river together. In an instant, the water sparkled with light, and the two pigs rose from the river transformed—radiant and winged, now angels just as the mysterious figure had promised.

They looked around, laughing and twirling in the air—but soon noticed something was missing. "Where's our friend?" one of them asked.

They turned and saw him still standing by the edge of the hill, unchanged and still a pig, his face filled with regret.

"Why didn't you jump?" they asked gently.

"I didn't believe her," he replied quietly. "I thought it wasn't real."

One of the new angels flew closer and said with kindness, "But think about it—what did you have to lose? If it wasn't true, you would've still been a pig. But what if it was true?" She smiled. "Now you'll never know what could've been."

The third pig looked down at the water, silent and thoughtful, as the sun finally set behind him.

MORAL

When there's nothing
to lose, taking a chance
can be the smartest
thing you do.
Sometimes, a small
leap of faith could
open the door to
something extraordinary.

8 CHAIN OF THOUGHTS

Once upon a time, in a small village near the edge of a forest, there lived a baby elephant.

He was full of life, energy, and a curious spirit. From the moment he was captured by humans, he longed to return to the wild. But the trainers had other plans. They tied one of his legs to a heavy iron chain fastened to a strong post.

The little elephant tugged and pulled with all his might, day after day, trying to break free. He used every ounce of his strength, but the chain was just too strong for him. Every time he tried to escape, he was met with harsh words and even harsher beatings.

The pain, both physical and emotional, became part of his reality.

Eventually, the baby elephant stopped trying. He came to believe something very powerful—and very wrong: he could never break free.

Years passed. The baby grew into a majestic, powerful elephant. Strong enough to topple trees and carry logs that weighed hundreds of kilos. But something curious happened—he was still tied, not with a thick iron chain, but with a simple piece of rope.

A rope so weak that he could easily snap it with a single tug. And yet, he didn't. He never even tried.

Why?

Because deep in his mind, he still believed what he had learned as a baby: "I can't break free." He was trapped not by the rope, but by the invisible chains of his past experience.

Moral of the Story:

We often carry beliefs from the past—beliefs that once protected us or made sense when we were weaker or smaller. But those same beliefs can hold us back even when we've grown far beyond them.

The real chains are not always physical—they are often in our minds.

Let go of what no longer serves you. You are stronger now.

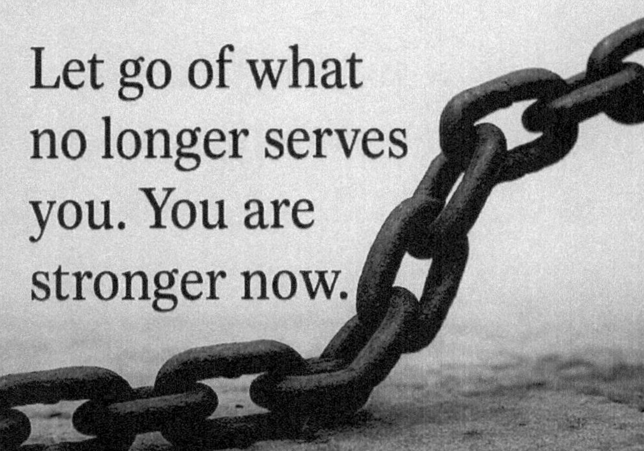

THE COCONUT SELLER'S JOURNEY

There was once a simple coconut seller who made his living in a small town. Day in and day out, he sat under a tree by the roadside, selling fresh coconuts to passing travelers. Life was simple, and he never ventured beyond the borders of his own town.

One day, some fellow traders told him, "There's a town not far from here where many visitors come every day. You should try selling your coconuts there—you'll make better money."

The idea struck him like a spark. "Why not?" he thought.

The next morning, he loaded up his cart with as many coconuts as it could carry and set off on the new adventure.

As he traveled down unfamiliar paths, he came to a fork in the road. Confused and unsure which way to go, he spotted a man walking by and called out, "Excuse me, do you know how to reach the nearby town with many visitors?"

The man nodded kindly. "Yes, I go there often. You have two options," he explained. "The road on the left is shorter—just 5 kilometers. But it's rough, full of mud and stones, and will take you about 45 minutes with that cart. The road on the right is longer—10 kilometers—but it's smooth, well-paved, and you'll reach in just 30 minutes. My advice is to take the right road."

The coconut seller looked at him, laughed, and said mockingly, "Why would I go 10 kilometers when I can reach in 5? You don't understand travel. I'm not wasting time!" And with that, he pulled his cart toward the left path.

At first, the journey seemed fine. But soon, the road turned bumpy. Thick mud clung to the wheels, sharp stones slowed him down, and more than once, his coconuts rolled off the cart and scattered. Each time, he had to stop, gather them all back, and push forward with even more effort.

By the time he reached the town, over 70 minutes had passed. He was exhausted, his cart was a mess, and the coconuts were dusty and bruised. As he wiped the sweat from his forehead, he remembered the man's words—and realized how wrong he had been to ignore the advice.

Moral of the Story:
When someone who knows
the path gives you advice,
don't be too proud to listen.
Experience speaks louder than
guesswork.
Sometimes the longer way is
the smarter way.
So hush, listen, and trust—
don't always try to outsmart
wisdom.

The sun was hot, and the desert seemed to go on forever. A lone traveler walked slowly, tired and thirsty. His lips were dry, and his legs were weak. He had been walking for days with no water left — only one small bottle.

Just when he thought he couldn't go any further, he saw something ahead. At first, he thought it was a dream. But as he got closer, he saw it was real — an old hand pump standing alone in the sand.

There was a wooden sign tied to it. The words were hard to read, but he made them out:

"This pump will give you water. But first, you must pour water into it to make it work. Look under the white rock — there's a bottle of water. Use it for the pump. Don't drink it first. Trust the pump."

The traveler looked under the rock and found the bottle. It was small, but the water inside looked clean and cool.

He held it in his hands and thought, "Should I drink it now and stay safe? What if the pump doesn't work? I'll lose everything."

But then another thought came: "What if it does work? What if there's more water waiting?"

He took a deep breath, opened the bottle, and poured the water into the pump.

At first, nothing happened. He started to worry.

Then he pushed the handle again… and again… and suddenly, cold water came rushing out!

He smiled, laughed, and cried all at once. He drank as much as he could, washed his face, and filled his own bottle. Before he left, he refilled the hidden bottle and put it back under the rock, just like he found it.

Then, under the old sign, he carved a few simple words: "It works. Just trust it."

Moral

Faith means giving even when you're not sure it will work out. Sometimes, you have to let go of what you have… to get something even better.

Trust the process, even if nothing happens at first.

In a peaceful valley near a quiet pond, a little eagle was raised among ducks. His egg had fallen from a cliffside nest during a storm and rolled down to the soft grass near the pond, where a kind mother duck found it. Not knowing it was different, she tucked it in with her own eggs. When the egg hatched, the eaglet was larger, with sharp eyes and strong wings —but he waddled, swam, and quacked just like his duck siblings. The other ducklings teased him now and then:

"You walk funny!" "Your wings are too big!" But the little eagle just smiled and tried harder to fit in.

Every morning, he joined the ducks in the pond, splashing about and saying, "Quack-quack!" even though it never quite sounded right coming from him. One day, as the little eagle was waddling along the pond's edge, a mighty shadow passed overhead. The ducks scattered in fear, flapping and diving into the water. The little eagle looked up.

High above soared a majestic eagle— wings wide, eyes sharp, riding the wind like a king.

The great eagle circled once and then descended, landing on a nearby tree. His voice was deep and calm:

"You there—young one. Why are you down here quacking with ducks?"

The little eagle blinked. "Because I am a duck!

Quack-quack!" he said proudly.

The big eagle tilted his head. "No, you're not. You're one of us. An eagle. You were born to fly, not waddle. To soar above mountains, not paddle in ponds."

But the little eagle shook his head. "I've always been here. I eat like them, walk like them, swim like them. I quack like them too!" He gave his best "quack," though it still came out more like a squeaky caw.

The big eagle smiled gently. "Just because you've lived among ducks doesn't mean you're one. Look at your wings. Look at your talons. You were made for the sky."

The little eagle looked at himself, then back at his duck friends splashing happily. Doubt crept into his heart. "But… what if I fall?"

The older eagle nodded with understanding. "You might. But falling is just part of learning to fly."

With that, the great eagle soared
back into the sky, disappearing
into the clouds.
The little eagle watched him go,
heart full of wonder, but fear still
clinging tightly. So he turned back
to the pond, back to his waddle,
and joined the ducks once again,
quacking quietly to himself.
But that night, he dreamed of
wind, cliffs, and skies without end.

Moral:

Even if the world tells you you're something you're not, the truth doesn't change. Sometimes, greatness calls us, but fear holds us back. Just because you're surrounded by ducks doesn't mean you're not an eagle. When someone sees the eagle in you, listen closely — one day, you'll be ready to fly.

12 SAINT AND GOD'S HELP

There was once a devout saint who lived in a small village. His faith in God was unwavering. He spent his days in prayer, guiding others in spiritual matters, and believed deeply that God would always protect him.

One year, heavy rains poured for days on end. Rivers swelled, and soon the village was threatened by a massive flood. As the water began to rise, people evacuated their homes. Some villagers came to the saint in a small boat and urged him, "Please come with us! The water is rising fast!"

The saint smiled gently and replied, "No, thank you. I have faith. God will save me." The villagers left reluctantly, and the water continued to rise. Later, another rescue team came in a larger boat. "Sir, you must come now! The floodwaters are reaching dangerous levels!"

But again, the saint refused. "I appreciate your concern, but I believe in God's plan. He will deliver me."

Eventually, the water engulfed his house. The saint climbed onto the roof. A helicopter flew overhead and dropped a rope ladder. The rescuers shouted, "Grab the ladder! This is your last chance!"

Still, the saint refused. "No need. I trust God completely. He will come to my rescue."

Tragically, the floodwaters surged higher, and the saint was swept away and drowned.

When he reached heaven, the saint stood before God, confused and heartbroken. "Lord," he asked, "I trusted You. Why didn't You save me?"

God looked at him with compassion and said, "My child, I did try to save you. I sent you two boats and a helicopter."

Moral:

Help from God or life may not always come in the way you expect. Be open to the forms in which assistance arrives. Faith is important, but so is recognizing the opportunities that come your way.

TEST OF TRUE FAITH

In a quiet village by the river, there lived a respected religious man known for his wisdom and devotion. Every day without fail, a humble farmer would send a pot of fresh milk to this man as an offering. Rain or shine, it arrived—carried by the farmer himself.

One day, the farmer fell seriously ill. Unable to make the daily journey, he called his young daughter to his side and said, "My child, no matter what happens, never let a day go by without delivering milk to the holy man. It is not just milk—it is our promise and faith."

The little girl nodded with innocent determination. From the next morning onward, she took on the responsibility with joy and devotion.

Days passed. Then one day, the skies darkened. A fierce storm swept across the village. The river overflowed and began flooding the paths, turning streets into swirling streams. The village panicked and took shelter.

But the little girl, with the milk pot balanced carefully on her head, stepped out into the storm.

Meanwhile, the religious man stood at his porch, watching the chaos. Suddenly, through the sheets of rain, he saw a tiny figure approaching—walking across the flooded river as if it were dry land. His eyes widened in disbelief. It was the little girl, calm and steady, unshaken by the raging waters.

When she arrived, he asked in astonishment, "Child, how did you cross the river like that? You walked on water!"

She smiled innocently and said, "My father told me never to miss bringing the milk. I remembered what you used to tell him: 'In any difficulty, just take my name and have faith—nothing will stop you.' So I took your name, trusted God, and walked."

The religious man was overwhelmed. "If you can do it with such simple faith, surely I can too," he said proudly.

He walked to the riverbank, looked up to the heavens, and was about to step into the water. But just before he did, he hesitated. Carefully, he reached down and pulled up his dhoti to keep it from getting wet. The girl watched quietly.

The moment his heart shifted from faith to fear—even a little—the river showed no mercy. He stepped in... and sank.

Moral

Faith is not in the words we preach or the rituals we follow—it's in the purity of trust, the surrender of doubt. The girl believed completely. The man doubted slightly. And that made all the difference.

In a dry and dusty land, there lived a small tribe that often struggled with long spells of drought. Their crops wilted, rivers ran shallow, and the people waited for the skies to show mercy.

But whenever hope seemed to fade, the tribe would turn to their rainmaker—a quiet, humble man with deep eyes and an ageless spirit. Every time the rains were needed, he would step into the open land, barefoot and focused, and begin to dance.

His movements were steady, his rhythm constant, and his presence unwavering. He danced under the hot sun. He danced through the cold wind. He danced when others doubted. And eventually—sometimes in hours, sometimes in days—the clouds would gather, and the rain would fall.

Other tribes heard of this and came to him in awe. "What is your secret?" they asked. "How is it that your rituals never fail? Do you know special chants or possess some ancient magic?"

The rainmaker simply smiled and said, "There is no secret. I just dance until it rains."

They blinked, surprised. "That's it?"

He nodded. "Yes. I dance with full belief. I never stop halfway. I don't wonder if it will rain—I keep dancing until it does."

Moral

Success often lies not in secret techniques, but in unwavering persistence. True power comes from not giving up—perseverance turns effort into results, and patience into miracles.

15.
GOD INDRA
– NO RAIN

Once upon a time, in a land where life depended entirely on the rains, the skies turned silent. Lord Indra, the god of rain, was displeased with the way humans had become careless and arrogant. In his disappointment, he made a powerful proclamation: "There shall be no rain for the next twelve years!"

The news struck the village like thunder. The rivers began to dry, the lakes shrank, and fear spread among the people. With no rain in sight, farming became impossible.

The villagers lost hope and turned to other trades—some became merchants, others moved away to find work. The once-busy farmlands lay barren and forgotten.

Yet, amidst this despair, one farmer stood out.

Every single day, this farmer would wake up at dawn, take his young son by the hand, and head to their empty, cracked field. With no water in sight and under a scorching sun, he would plow the land, remove weeds, and prepare the soil—just as if the rain were coming tomorrow.

The villagers laughed and mocked him, "Why waste your time? Indra himself said there will be no rain for 12 years!"

The farmer smiled and replied calmly, "I'm not preparing for today. I'm preparing for the day after the rain returns. If I stop now, I'll forget how to farm. And when the rains do come, I won't be ready. But if I continue each day, I'll be prepared.

And my son will learn never to stop doing the right thing—rain or no rain."
High above, Lord Indra was watching. The farmer's unwavering faith, discipline, and quiet wisdom began to stir something within the rain god. He thought to himself, "If that man continues to farm without rain, just to keep his knowledge alive... what if I, too, forget how to bring the rains when the time comes?"
Moved by the farmer's dedication, Lord Indra reconsidered his decision. The very next day, dark clouds rolled in, thunder echoed through the skies, and rain poured down upon the land—soaking the earth, reviving the crops, and surprising the villagers.
The farmer and his son stood in the field, smiling. They were ready.

Moral

Consistency and preparation in the face of uncertainty is true wisdom. Don't wait for the perfect conditions—do your part every day. The world may change its course for those who never stop doing what is right.

Ramprasad was a simple, honest man who had lived his entire life in a small town. Though he was content with his humble routine, he carried one dream close to his heart for as long as he could remember—to one day visit the great city of Mumbai. The city of dreams, lights, sea, and endless stories. Years passed, and the dream stayed just that—a dream. He never found the time or the opportunity to go. But one morning, everything changed.

His manager at work called him into the office. "Ramprasad," he said, "we need someone to go to Mumbai for some important company paperwork. The job is yours, and all arrangements are made—your train ticket is booked for tomorrow morning at 9 AM."

Ramprasad was overjoyed. His eyes sparkled like a child's. That night, he packed his modest bag, laid out his best clothes, and barely slept out of excitement.

The next morning, he reached the railway station well ahead of time—at 8 AM, an hour before departure. With an hour to spare, he decided to walk around the platform and soak in the moment. That's when he spotted an old-fashioned coin-operated weight machine, the kind that also printed out a little card with your weight and a "fortune."

Feeling playful, he inserted a coin and stepped on it. The card popped out almost instantly. But when he read it, his jaw dropped.

"Your name is Ramprasad.
Your weight is 79 kg.
Your train to Mumbai is at 9 AM."

He blinked. How could the machine know his name, weight, and train time? Was it magic? Or a prank?

Determined to test it, he tried again—this time wearing his jacket inside out. Same result. He rubbed mud on his face to disguise himself and tried again. Same result. He borrowed a cap from a vendor and returned. Still the same.

Frustrated but now obsessed, Ramprasad tried everything. He tore parts of his clothing, smudged his face, even went to the station barber and got a quick, rough haircut just to look different.

Finally, he returned to the machine one last time. He inserted the coin and stared at the card as it printed. This time, it read:
"Your name is Ramprasad.
Your weight is 79 kg.
Your train to Mumbai was at 9 AM.
And… it's gone."
Ramprasad's heart sank. He looked at the clock—it was 9:15 AM.
The train had left.
In chasing a mystery, he had lost his moment.

Moral:

When life gives you a chance to chase your dreams, stay focused. Don't let distractions —no matter how fascinating— pull you away from your path. Dreams come true for those who keep their eyes on the destination, not those who lose time in curiosity and doubt.

Father Michael was a devoted man — soft-spoken, humble, and committed to serving God. For over forty years, he had stood at the altar every Sunday, delivering sermons to the faithful. Though his voice was calm and his words sincere, he often noticed his congregation drifting off mid-sermon. He would smile gently and continue, believing that simply being present was enough.

One stormy night, after a late-night prayer meeting, Father Michael stood outside the church, clutching his worn Bible. It was pouring, and few cars were on the road.

Finally, a taxi screeched to a stop in front of him.

The driver, a rough-looking man with an unshaven face and loud music blaring from the radio, waved him in. "Hop in, Padre!" he said, flashing a mischievous grin.

Father Michael hesitated but climbed in, too tired to wait any longer.

From the moment the wheels turned, the ride was chaos. The driver sped through puddles, skidded around corners, and wove between cars like he was in a race.

Father Michael gripped the seat, his knuckles white, muttering prayers under his breath.

"Are you trying to kill us?" he asked, voice trembling.

"Nah, relax! I've been doing this for years," the driver said, chuckling. "No one's died on my watch—yet!"

But fate had other plans.

A blinding flash, a screech of metal, and everything went silent.

When Father Michael opened his eyes, the storm was gone. The air was warm, golden light filled the sky, and a feeling of peace washed over him. He stood next to the taxi driver in front of Heaven's gates.

Saint Peter approached them, smiling. "Welcome, children of Earth."

He turned to the taxi driver first. "You — come with me. You've earned a mansion in paradise. Here are your keys. It's got a garden, a view of the Celestial River, and a golden driveway. Enjoy eternity."

The driver let out a whistle. "Sweet!"

Father Michael smiled, expecting a similar reward. After all, he had served the Church his whole life.

But then Saint Peter handed him a modest key. "Father Michael, your cottage is just down that path. Peaceful, quiet, right beside the Chapel of Eternal Light."

Father Michael blinked. "Wait… a cottage? I was a priest! I served God for decades! He drove like a maniac!"

Saint Peter nodded with a chuckle. "Yes, but when you preached… people dozed off. When he drove… even you prayed."

Moral

It's not always about what you intend to do. It's about the impact you make.

Once upon a time in a small village, there lived a blind man who had never seen the world nor tasted many of its sweet delights. He was known to be quite skeptical and cautious, often questioning everything that came his way.

One warm afternoon, a kind-hearted man from the neighborhood was passing by with a pot of freshly made kheer—a delicious, sweet rice pudding made with milk, sugar, and dry fruits. The aroma was heavenly, and it drifted through the air, catching the attention of everyone around, including the blind man.

The kind man noticed the blind man sitting under a tree and felt moved by compassion. He walked over and said, "Brother, would you like to taste some of this delicious kheer? It's freshly made, and I'd be happy to share it with you." The blind man raised his eyebrows. "Kheer?" he asked. "What is that?" "It's a sweet dish," the man replied, smiling. "Made with rice, milk, sugar, cardamom, and garnished with dry fruits like almonds and raisins. It's a treat!" But instead of accepting it, the blind man grew suspicious. "Milk, you say? Where did the milk come from? Was the cow healthy? And rice… is it clean? What kind of sugar did you use? I've heard sugar can be harmful. And what if the dry fruits are stale? How do I know it's safe?"

The kind man patiently answered every question. But the more he explained, the more questions the blind man asked. "What if your hands were dirty while making it? And what if the kheer is poisoned? How can I trust what I cannot see?"

The man tried to reassure him, "I understand your concern, but I made it with care and love. Just take one bite—you'll know it for yourself."

But the blind man shook his head. "No, I need to know everything before I put it in my mouth."

Finally, the kind man sighed. "Alright then. If you do not wish to taste it, I won't force you."

And with that, he took the pot of kheer and walked away, sharing it with others who welcomed it with smiles and gratitude.

The blind man sat under the tree, empty-handed, his mouth watering, and a strange emptiness growing in his heart. He had let his doubts rob him of an experience—a taste he had never known and might never be offered again.

Moral

Sometimes, overthinking and doubt can keep us from enjoying the beautiful experiences life offers. It's good to ask questions—but not at the cost of missing out on the sweetness of life.

19
THE LOST CHILD

Once upon a time, in a peaceful valley surrounded by hills and rivers, there were two neighboring villages— Sundarpur and Devgarh. For years, the two villages had lived side by side, but old grudges and misunderstandings had brewed bitterness between them.

One day, a small disagreement over water from a shared river turned into a fiery argument. Voices rose, tempers flared, and soon a heated fight broke out between the people of both villages.

In the chaos, as people shouted and threw stones, a small boy from Sundarpur—barely five years old—got lost in the crowd. In a cruel twist, some hot-headed men from Devgarh took the boy with them while retreating, thinking it might give them an advantage in future negotiations.

The boy's mother, Meera, searched frantically through the dust and smoke. Her heart sank when she realized her child was missing. As the fighting stopped and the villagers gathered to tend to the wounded, she cried out in anguish, "They've taken my child! Someone help me!"

The villagers were moved by her pain. A few brave men stood up and said, "We'll go get your son back, Meera. Don't worry." She folded her hands and wept in gratitude. The group prepared for the journey. But instead of rushing, they began slowly.

Some packed food, others sharpened sticks and made torches. They chatted, rested, and took their time. The sun began to set as they finally started walking toward Devgarh. By the time they were halfway, night had fallen. "We'll camp here," one of them said. "We can't march into their village in the dark. Let's eat and rest. We'll go at dawn."

They lit a fire, cooked dinner, shared stories, and fell asleep under the stars. But just before sunrise, a sound echoed through the quiet hills—a child's cry. Startled, the men woke up and followed the sound, hurrying through the fog. To their astonishment, they saw Meera—tired and dusty, but smiling—with her little boy clinging to her arms.

"You... you brought him back?" one of the men asked, still half-asleep.

Meera nodded, eyes filled with tears. "Yes. He is my child. I couldn't wait. I couldn't rest. I couldn't let fear or comfort stop me. While you were eating and sleeping, I followed the path, crawled through the fields, and snuck into their village in the dark. I heard him crying, found him, and brought him back."

The men stood in silence, ashamed and humbled by her courage and determination.

Moral

When something is truly yours, when your heart is in it, you don't wait for the perfect moment—you act with urgency, passion, and love.
Delays, doubts, and comfort-seeking often steal the opportunity to do what's right.
True commitment doesn't wait— it moves, even in the dark.

Closing Note
You've just walked through 19 stories, each carrying a seed of truth. May they bloom in your mind and heart, quietly guiding you through life's winding roads.
Keep telling stories. And more importantly — live one worth telling.

- Drafted with heart by SGMaxout

Shared
stories
ONBOARD TRAVEL JOURNAL
8